MEN'S EDITION

JAZZ BALLADS FOR

15 CLASSIC STANDARDS IN CUSTOM VOCAL ARRANGEMENTS

On the recordings:
Steve Rawlins, piano; Jim DeJulio, bass; Gordon Peeke, drums
Steve Rawlins, producer; Andy Waterman, engineer

To access companion recorded jazz trio accompaniments online, visit:
www.halleonard.com/mylibrary
Enter Code
1538-6202-1704-8174

This publication is not for sale in the EU.

ISBN 978-0-634-06457-9

HAL•LEONARD® CORPORATION

7777 W. BLUEMOUND RD. P.O. BOX 13819 MILWAUKEE, WI 53213

Visit Hal Leonard Online at
www.halleonard.com

Men's Key

Autumn In New York

Words and Music by Vernon Duke

Moderately

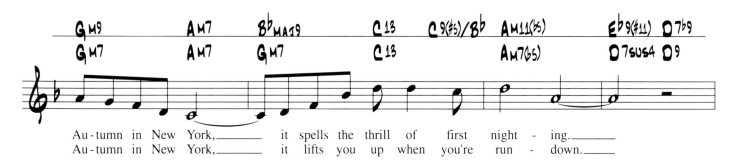

Au-tumn in New York,_____ why does it seem so in-vit ing?_____
Au-tumn in New York,_____ the gleam-ing roof-tops at sun - down._____

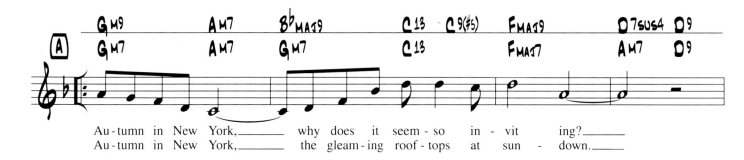

Au-tumn in New York,_____ it spells the thrill of first night - ing._____
Au-tumn in New York,_____ it lifts you up when you're run - down._____

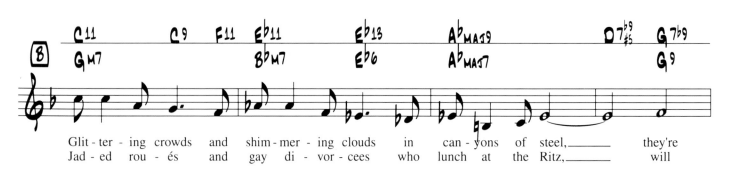

Glit-ter-ing crowds and shim-mer-ing clouds in can-yons of steel,_____ they're
Jad-ed rou-és and gay di-vor-cees who lunch at the Ritz,_____ will

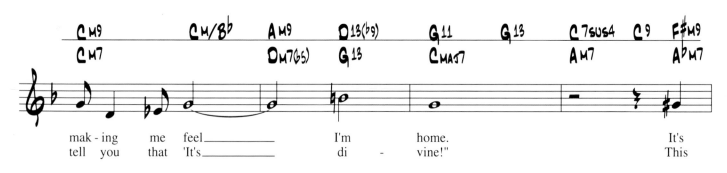

mak-ing me feel_____ I'm home. It's
tell you that 'It's_____ di - vine!" This

3

Men's Key

Do You Know What It Means To Miss New Orleans

Lyric by Eddie De Lange
Music by Louis Alter

Slowly

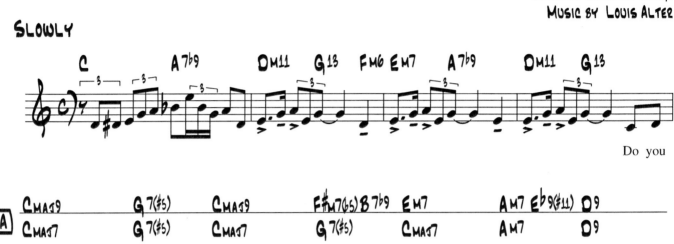

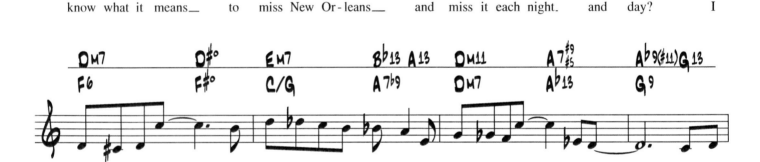

Men's Key

Ev'ry Time We Say Goodbye

Words and Music by Cole Porter

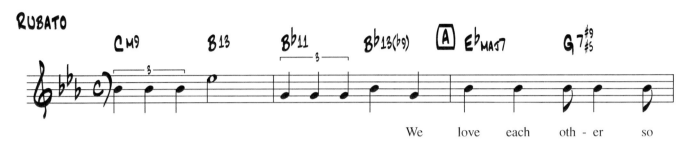

Rubato

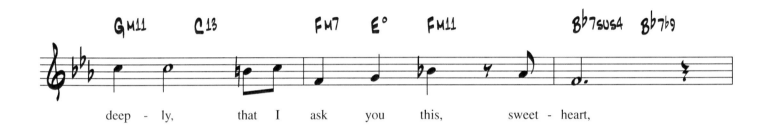

We love each oth-er so

deep-ly, that I ask you this, sweet-heart,

why should we quar-rel ev-er, why can't we be e-nough

Moderate Tempo

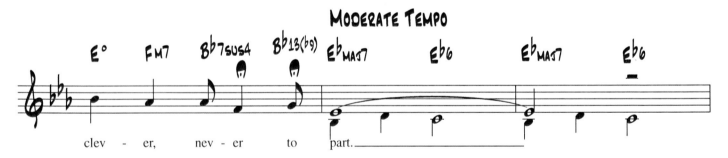

clev-er, nev-er to part.____

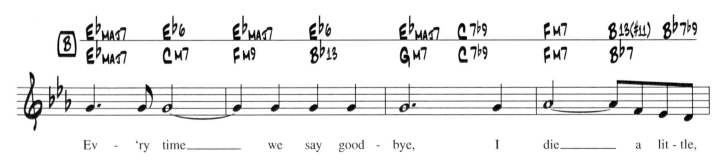

Ev-'ry time____ we say good-bye, I die____ a lit-tle,

Men's Key

Just One More Chance

Words by Sam Coslow
Music by Arthur Johnston

Rubato

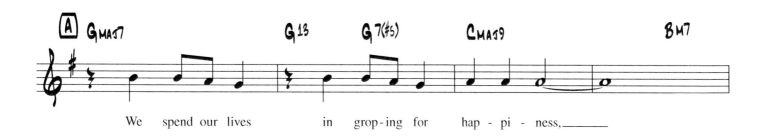

We spend our lives in grop-ing for hap-pi-ness,

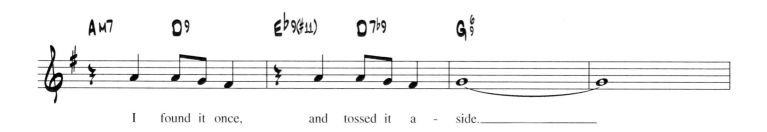

I found it once, and tossed it a-side.

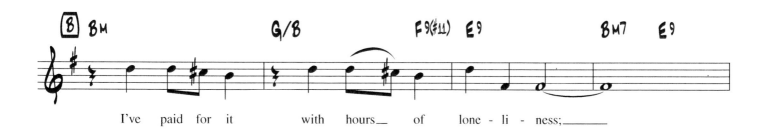

I've paid for it with hours of lone-li-ness;

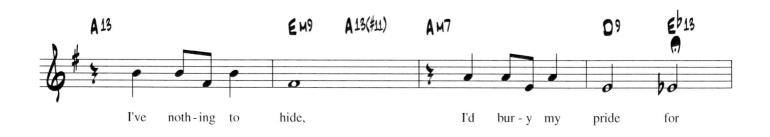

I've noth-ing to hide, I'd bur-y my pride for

MODERATELY

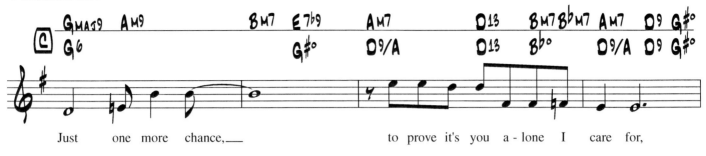

Just one more chance,___ to prove it's you a-lone I care for,

each night I say a lit-tle pray'r for just one more chance.___

Just one more night,___ to taste the kiss-es that en-chant me,

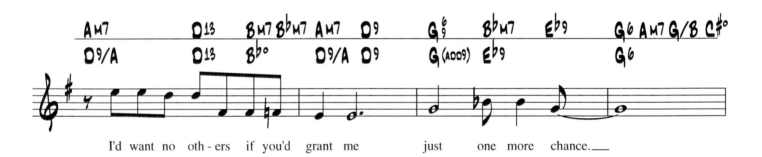

I'd want no oth-ers if you'd grant me just one more chance.___

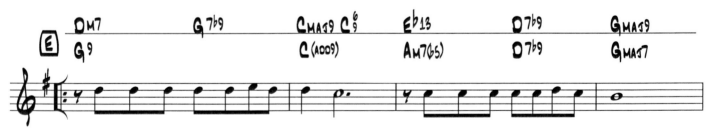

I've learned the mean-ing of re-pen-tance; now you're the ju-ry at my trial.

Men's Key

I Could Write a Book

Words by Lorenz Hart
Music by Richard Rodgers

Easy Swing

Men's Key

I Got It Bad and That Ain't Good

Words by Paul Francis Webster
Music by Duke Ellington

Men's Key
It Might As Well Be Spring

Lyrics by Oscar Hammerstein II
Music by Richard Rodgers

Moderately - Opt. Samba

Men's Key

Lush Life

Words and Music by Billy Strayhorn

Freely

used to vis-it all the ver-y gay plac-es,___ those come what may plac-es,___ where one re-

lax-es on the ax-is of the wheel of life_____ to get the

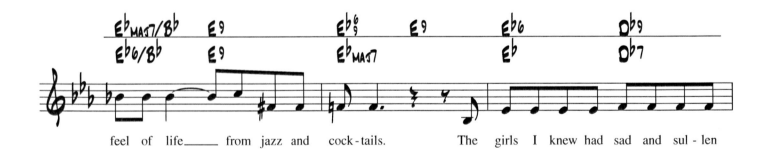

feel of life_____ from jazz and cock-tails. The girls I knew had sad and sul-len

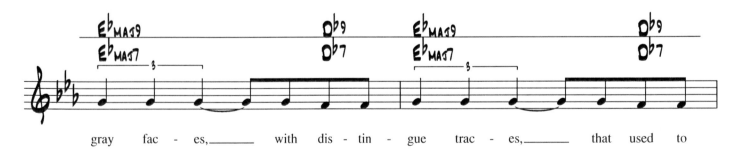

gray fac-es,_____ with dis-tin-gue trac-es,_____ that used to

be there you could see where they'd been washed a - way____ by too man - y

through the day twelve o' - clock tails. Then you came a - long with

your si - ren song to tempt me to mad - ness,____ I thought for a-while that

your poig - nant smile was tinged with the sad - ness of a great love for me.__

__ Ah, yes I was wrong,____

Men's Key

My Funny Valentine

Words by Lorenz Hart
Music by Richard Rodgers

Men's Key

My Romance

Words by Lorenz Hart
Music by Richard Rodgers

Men's Key

The Nearness Of You

from the Paramount Picture Romance in the Dark

Words by Ned Washington
Music by Hoagy Carmichael

27

Men's Key

Manhattan

Words by Lorenz Hart
Music by Richard Rodgers

Freely

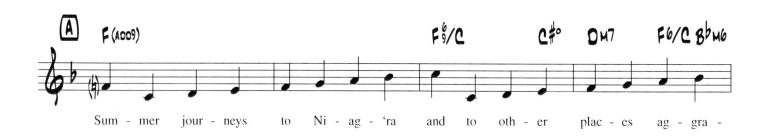

Sum - mer jour - neys to Ni - ag - 'ra and to oth - er plac - es ag - gra -

vate all our cares; we'll save our fares;

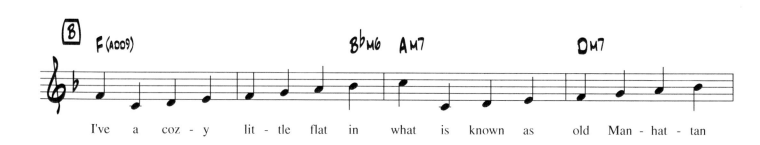

I've a coz - y lit - tle flat in what is known as old Man - hat - tan

we'll set - tle down right here in town:

Men's Key
A Nightingale Sang In Berkeley Square

Lyric by Eric Maschwitz
Music by Manning Sherwin

When true lov-ers meet in May-fair, so the le-gend tells;

song - birds sing, Win-ter turns to Spring._____

Ev-'ry wind-ing street in May-fair falls be-neath the spell. I

know such en-chant-ment can be,_____ 'cuz it hap-pened one eve-ning to me._____ That

Men's Key

Solitude

Words and Music by Duke Ellington,
Eddie De Lange and Irving Mills

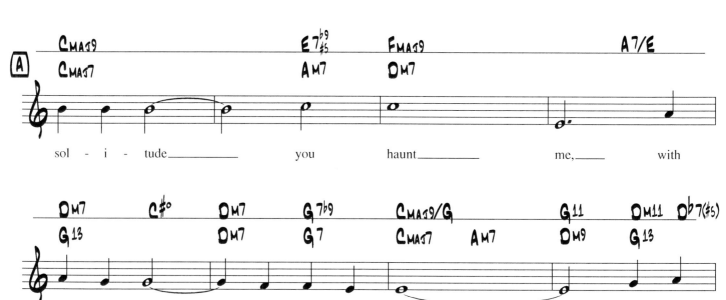

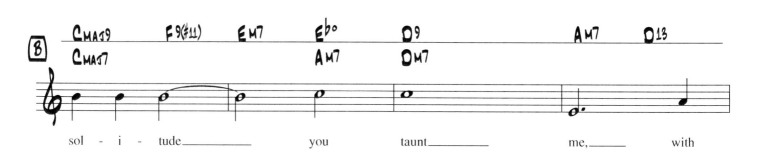

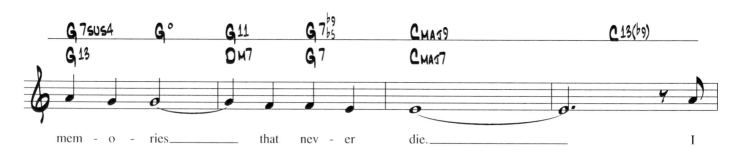

Men's Key

Stardust

Words by Mitchell Parish
Music by Hoagy Carmichael

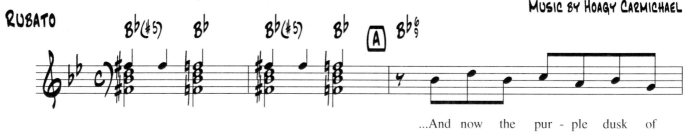

...And now the pur-ple dusk of

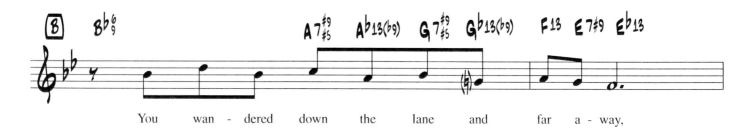

twi-light time   steals a-cross the mead-ows of my heart.   High up in the sky the

lit-tle stars climb,   Al-ways re-mind-ing me that we're a-part.

You wan-dered down the lane and far a-way,

leav-ing me a song that will not die.   Love is now the star-dust

of yes-ter-day,   the mu-sic of the years gone by._____ Some-times I

MODERATELY

38